How Cars Changed the World

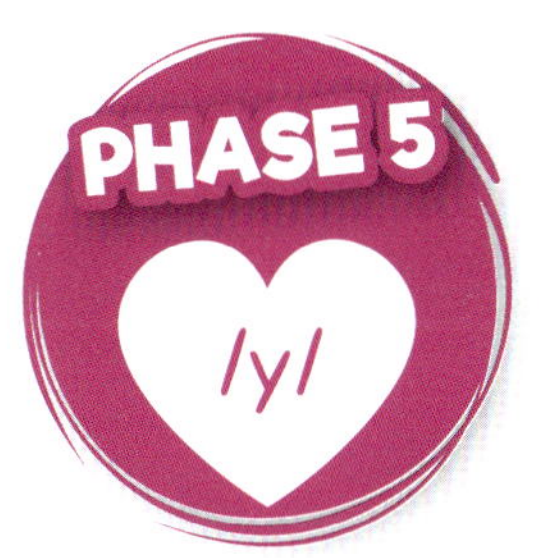

Level 8 – Purple

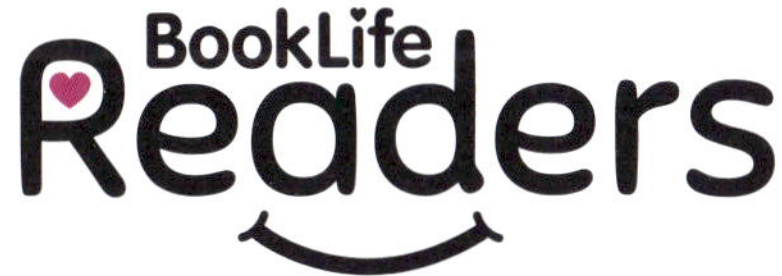

Helpful Hints for Reading at Home

The graphemes (written letters) and phonemes (units of sound) used throughout this series are aligned with Letters and Sounds. This offers a consistent approach to learning whether reading at home or in the classroom.

HERE IS A LIST OF PHONEMES FOR THIS PHASE OF LEARNING. AN EXAMPLE OF THE PRONUNCIATION CAN BE FOUND IN BRACKETS.

Phase 5			
ay (day)	ou (out)	ie (tie)	ea (eat)
oy (boy)	ir (girl)	ue (blue)	aw (saw)
wh (when)	ph (photo)	ew (new)	oe (toe)
au (Paul)	a_e (make)	e_e (these)	i_e (like)
o_e (home)	u_e (rule, cube)		

Phase 5 Alternative Pronunciations of Graphemes			
a (hat, what)	e (bed, she)	i (fin, find)	o (hot, so, other)
u (but, unit)	c (cat, cent)	g (got, giant)	ow (cow, blow)
ie (tied, field)	ea (eat, bread)	er (farmer, herb)	ch (chin, school, chef)
y (yes, by, very)	ou (out, shoulder, could, you)		

HERE ARE SOME WORDS WHICH YOUR CHILD MAY FIND TRICKY.

Phase 5 Tricky Words			
oh	their	people	Mr
Mrs	looked	called	asked
could			

TOP TIPS FOR HELPING YOUR CHILD TO READ:

- Allow children time to break down unfamiliar words into units of sound and then encourage children to string these sounds together to create the word.

- Encourage your child to point out any focus phonics when they are used.

- Read through the book more than once to grow confidence.

- Ask simple questions about the text to assess understanding.

- Encourage children to use illustrations as prompts.

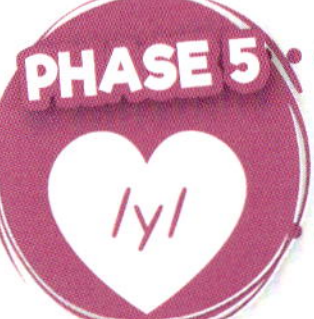

This book focuses on the alternative pronunciations of the grapheme /y/ and is a Purple level 8 book band.

Which of these words rhyme?

coffee

fly

welly

sky

very

Why do we invent new things? We invent new things to fix problems! When something new fixes a big problem, it can change the world.

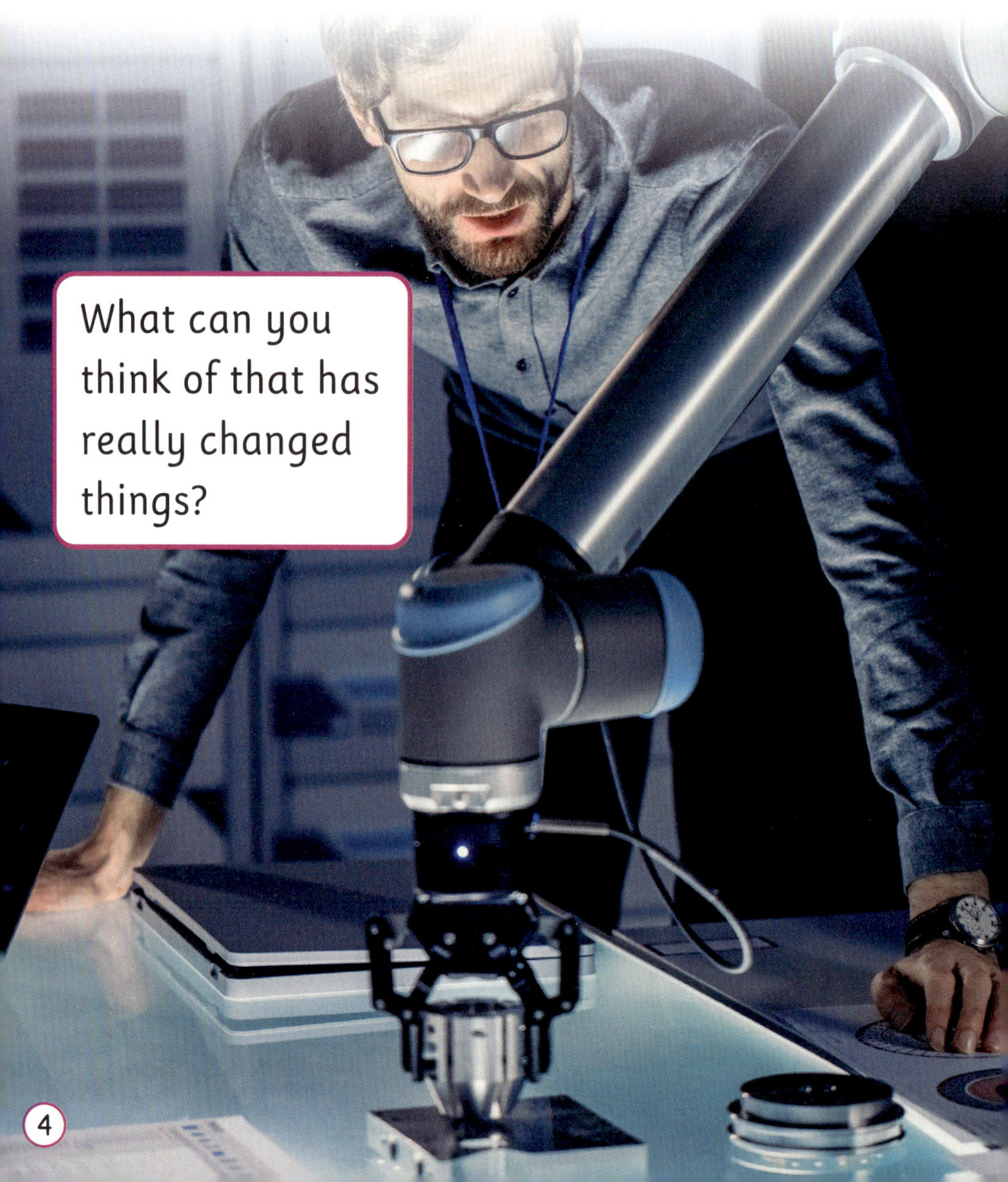

When cars were invented, they made the world feel smaller and connected people more than ever. Understanding the things we invent can help us understand the world around us a little better.

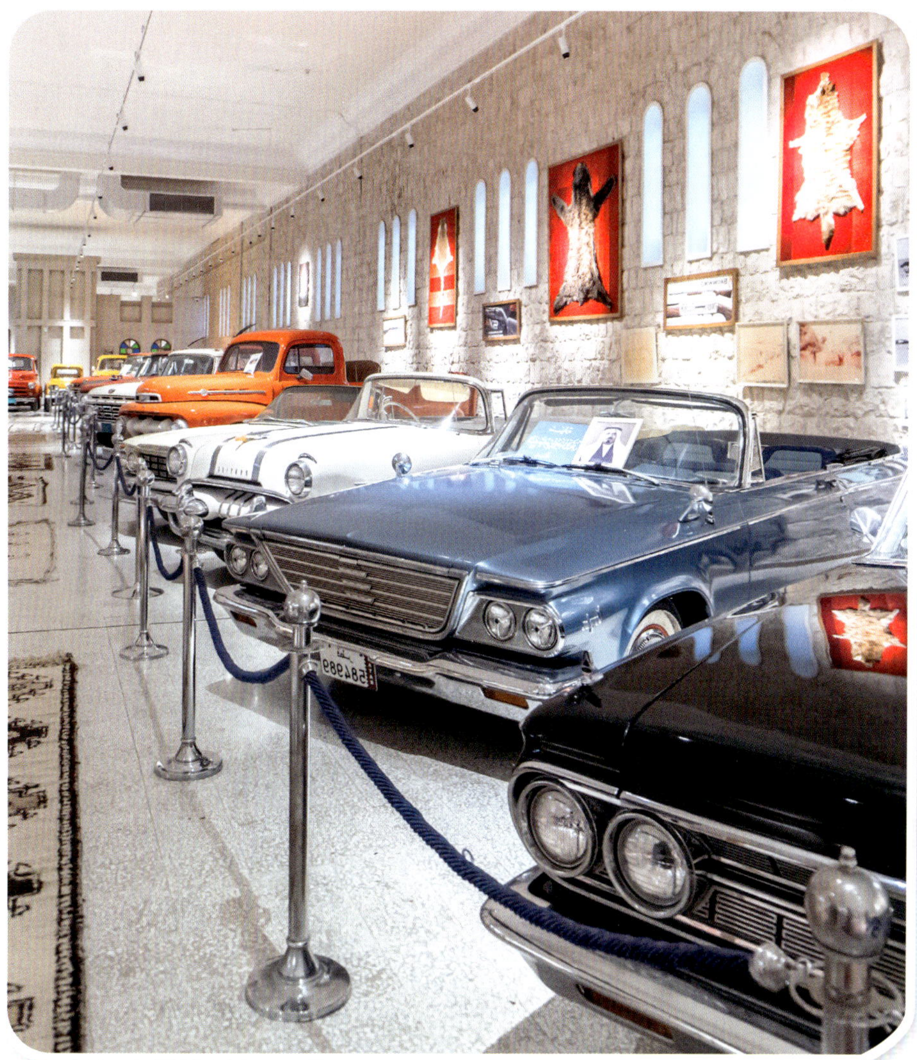

We have come a long way from the animal-drawn carts of our ancestors. The car has changed how we travel and made travel much easier than it was.

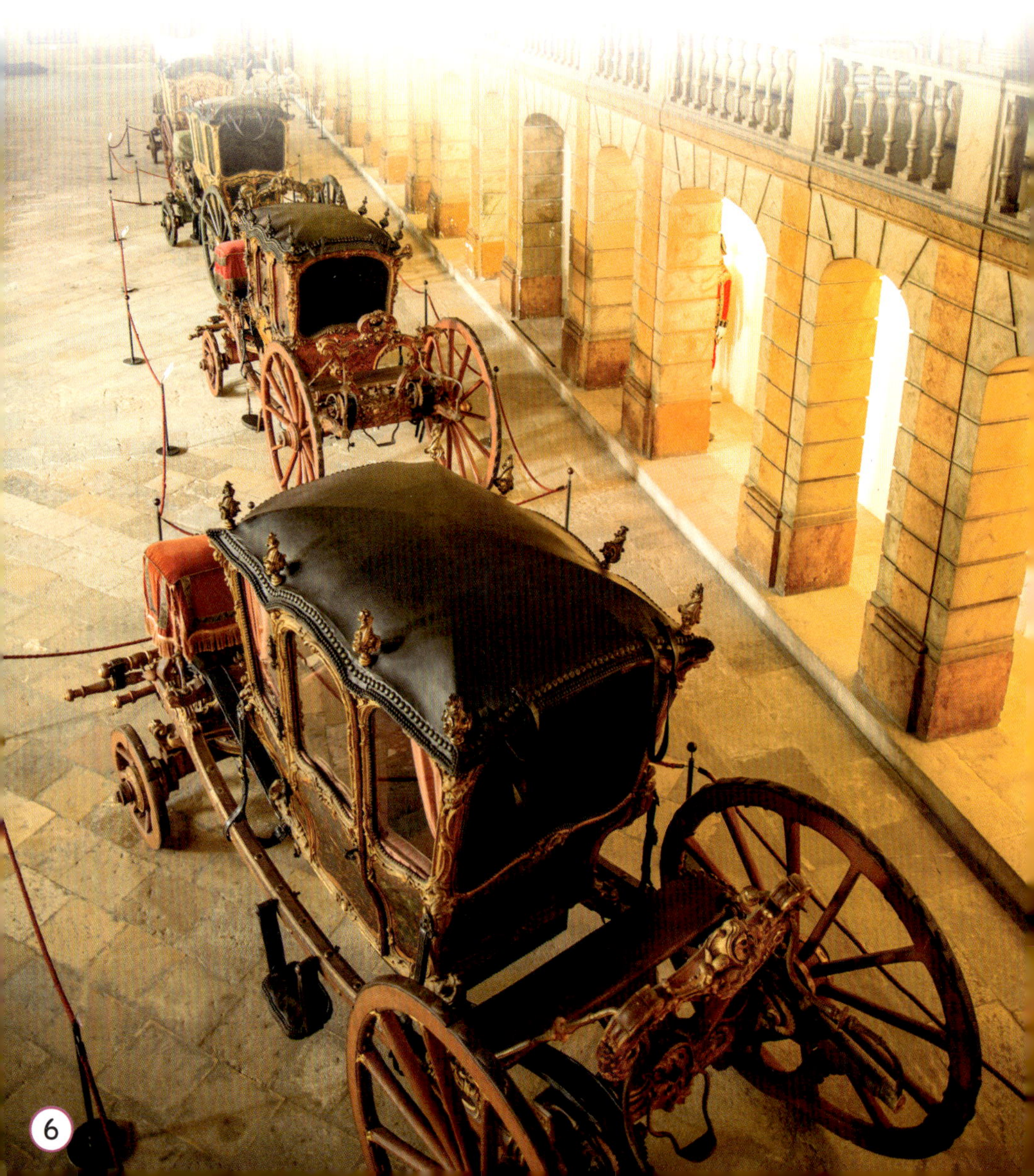

200 years ago, if you wanted to travel a long way to visit people for a nice day out, the trip could take up to 12 hours on a horse and cart!

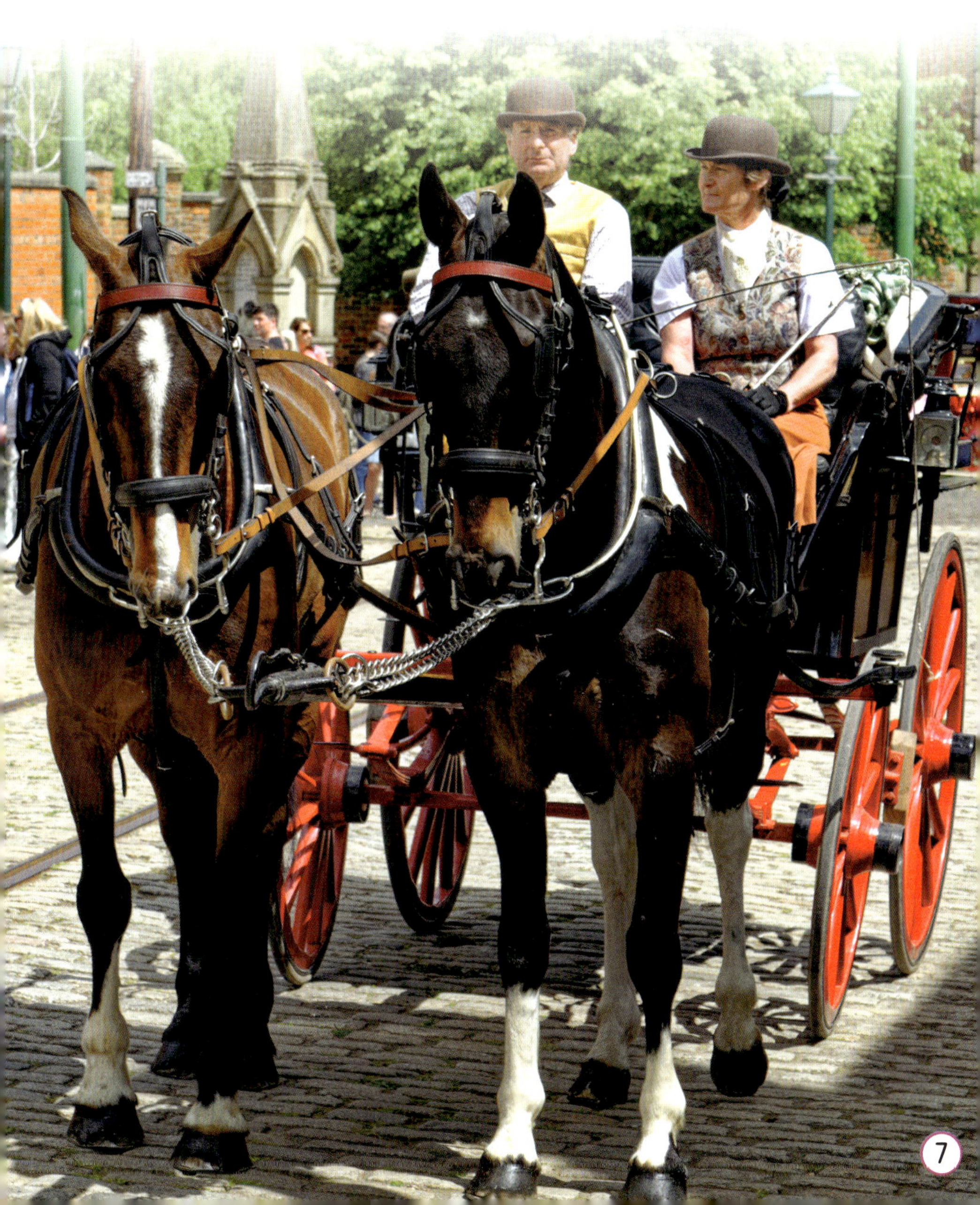

When cars were first introduced to America, most cars were powered by steam and electricity, instead of by petrol. But soon, petrol became the main fuel used to power cars.

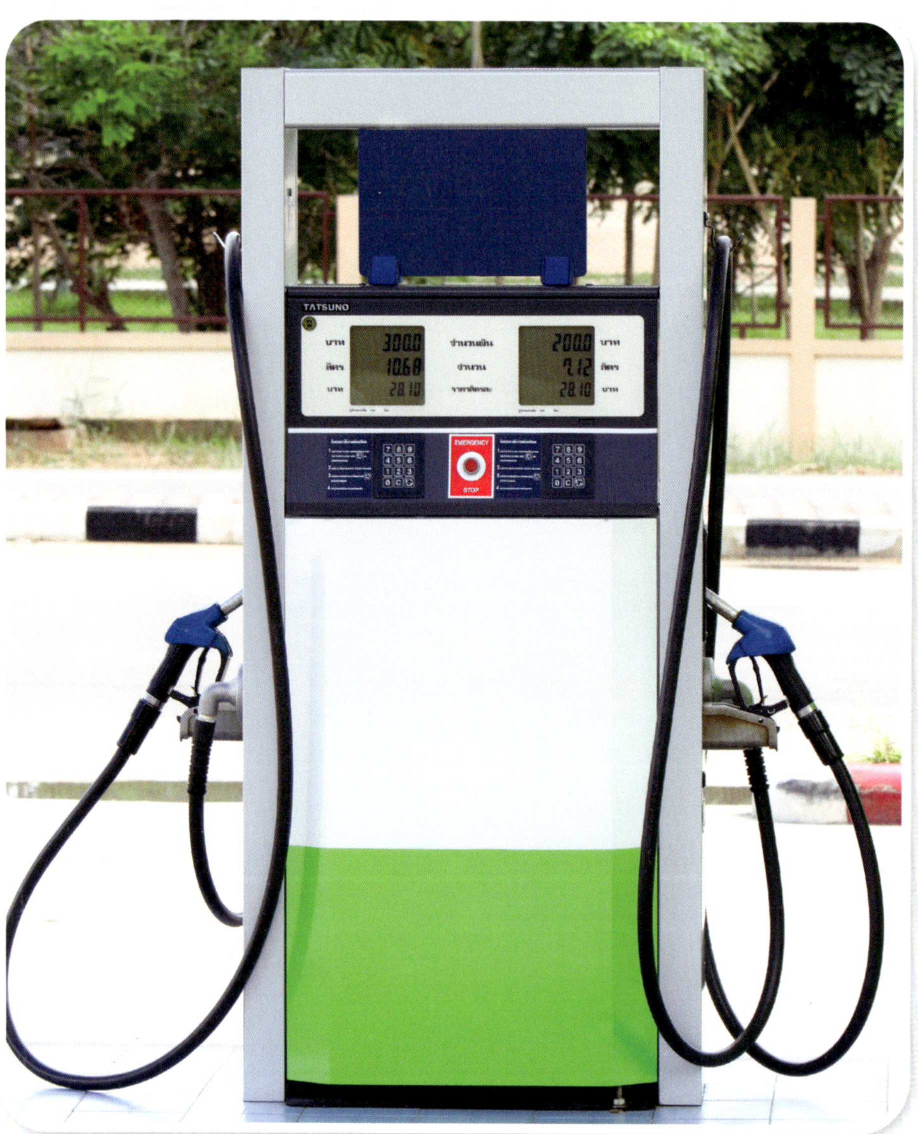

Even if early electric cars were popular, there was a big problem with them. Few towns or villages had electricity at this time.

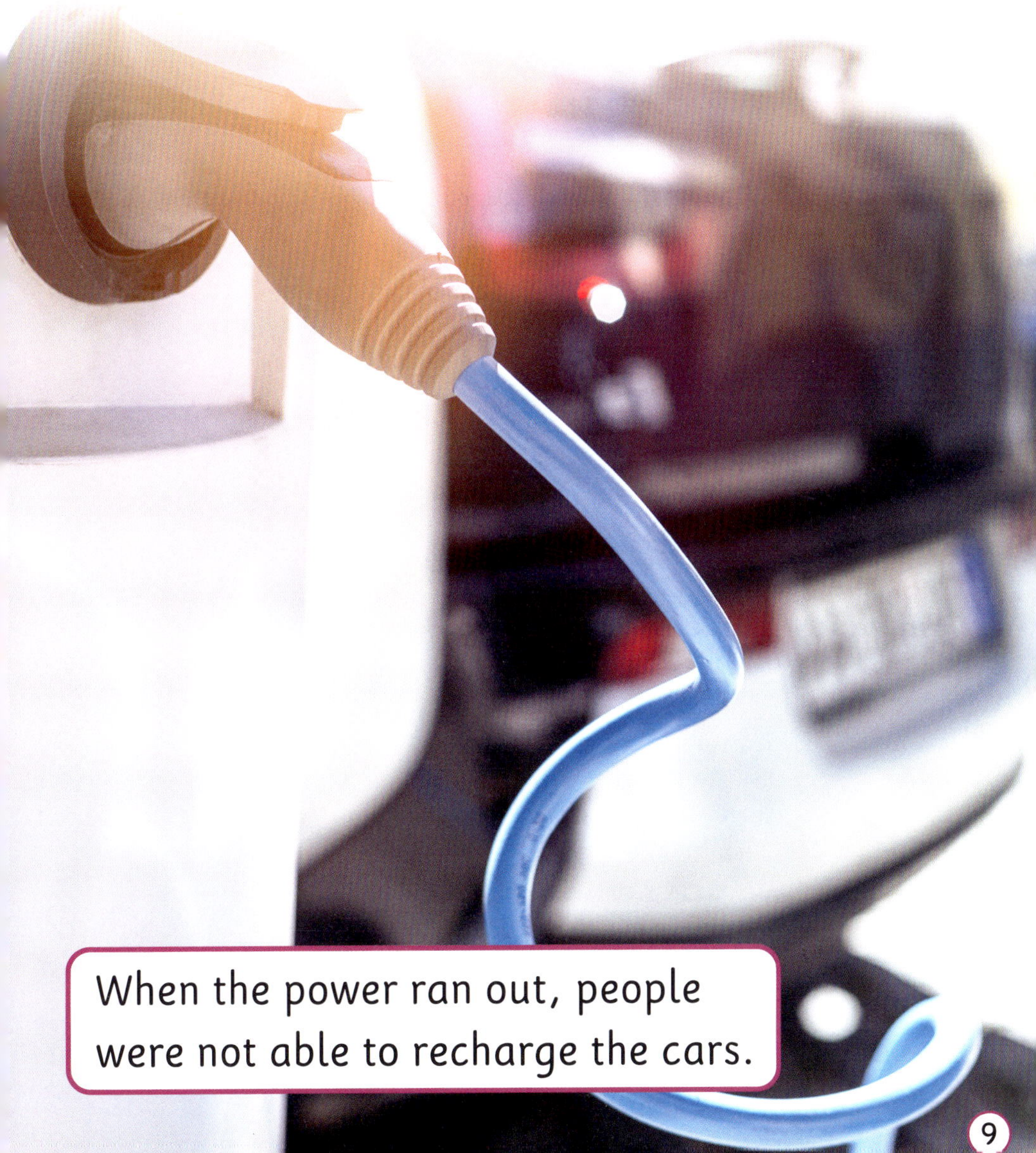

When the power ran out, people were not able to recharge the cars.

Henry Ford's petrol-based car, the Model T, put an end to cars powered by electricity. The Model T cost $650, while the electric roadster was a costly $1,750.

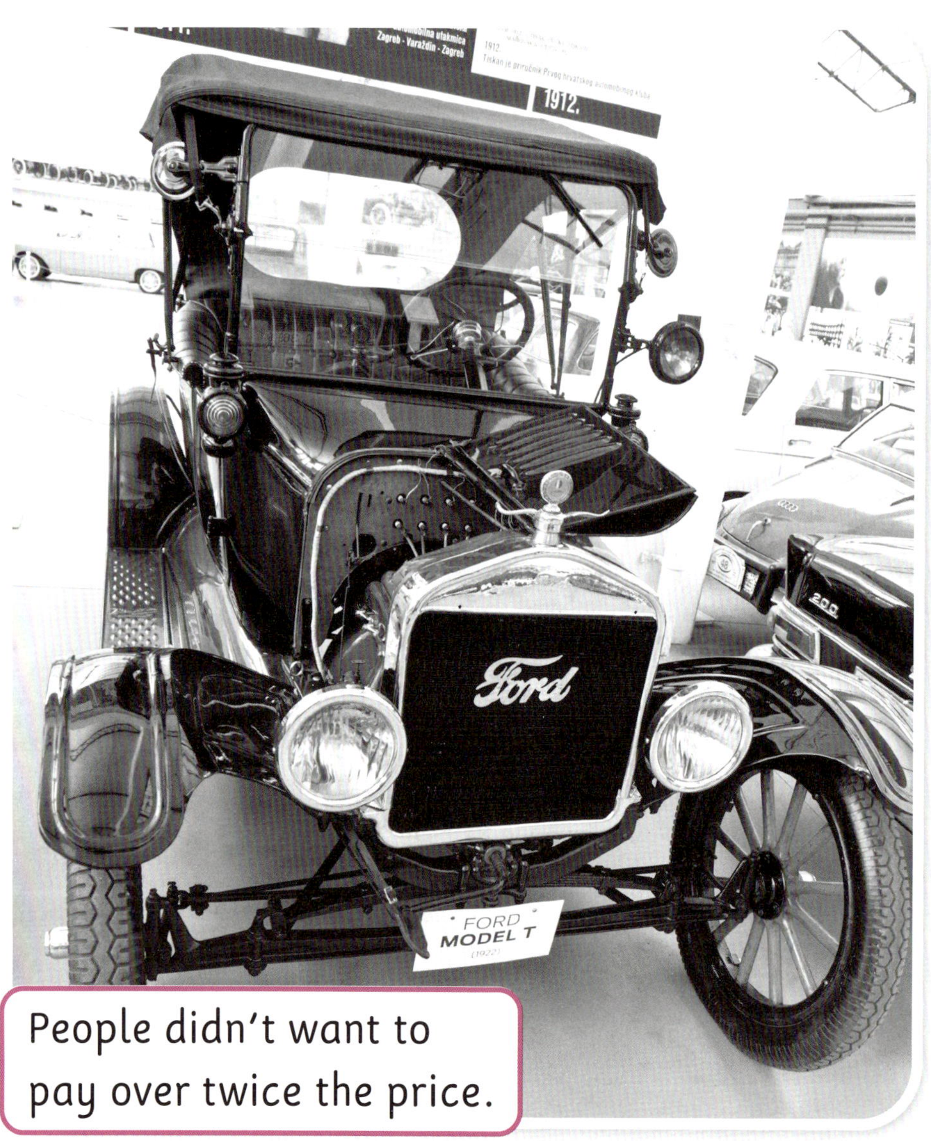

People didn't want to pay over twice the price.

The success of the Model T led to an increase in the use of crude oil to make fuel for cars. Oil and petrol became important, and more car companies started using it.

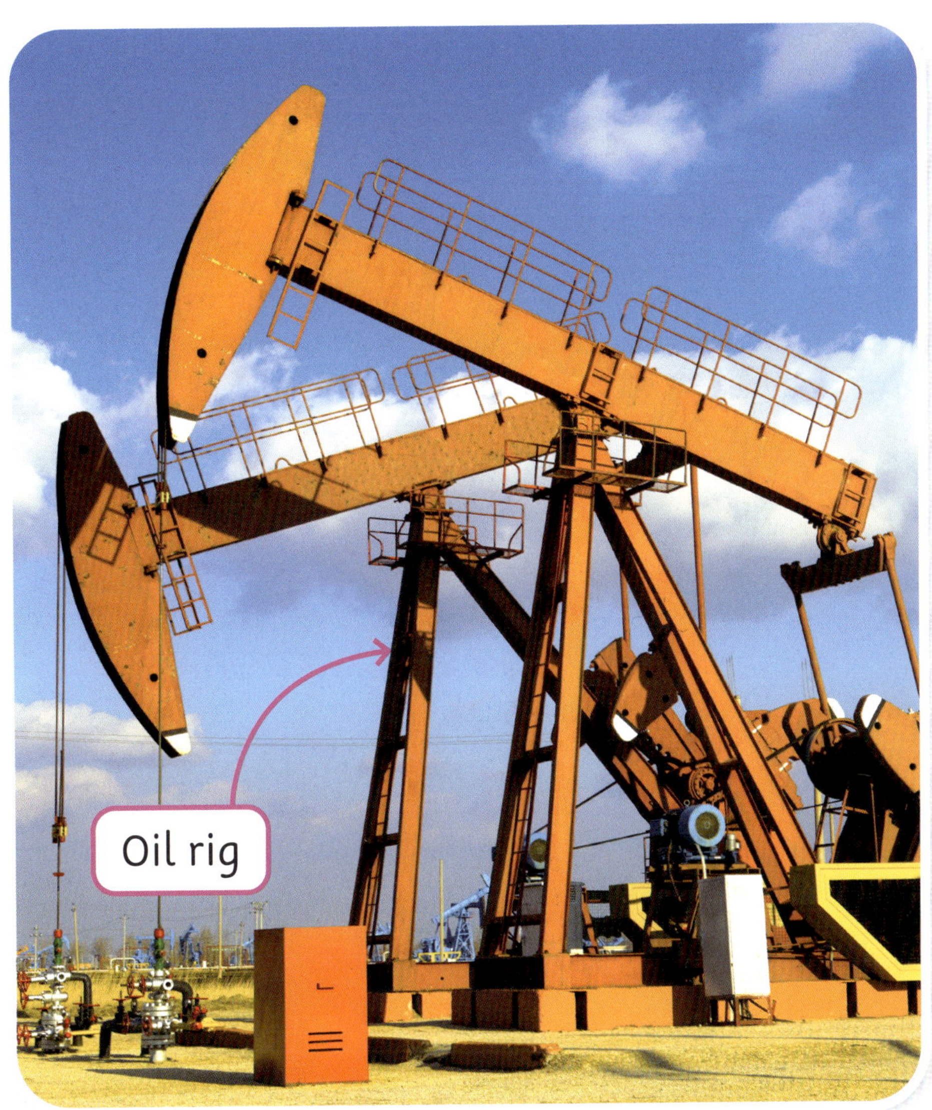

Henry Ford's Model T didn't just change which cars people got. Henry Ford changed the way people made cars with the very clever way the company made cars.

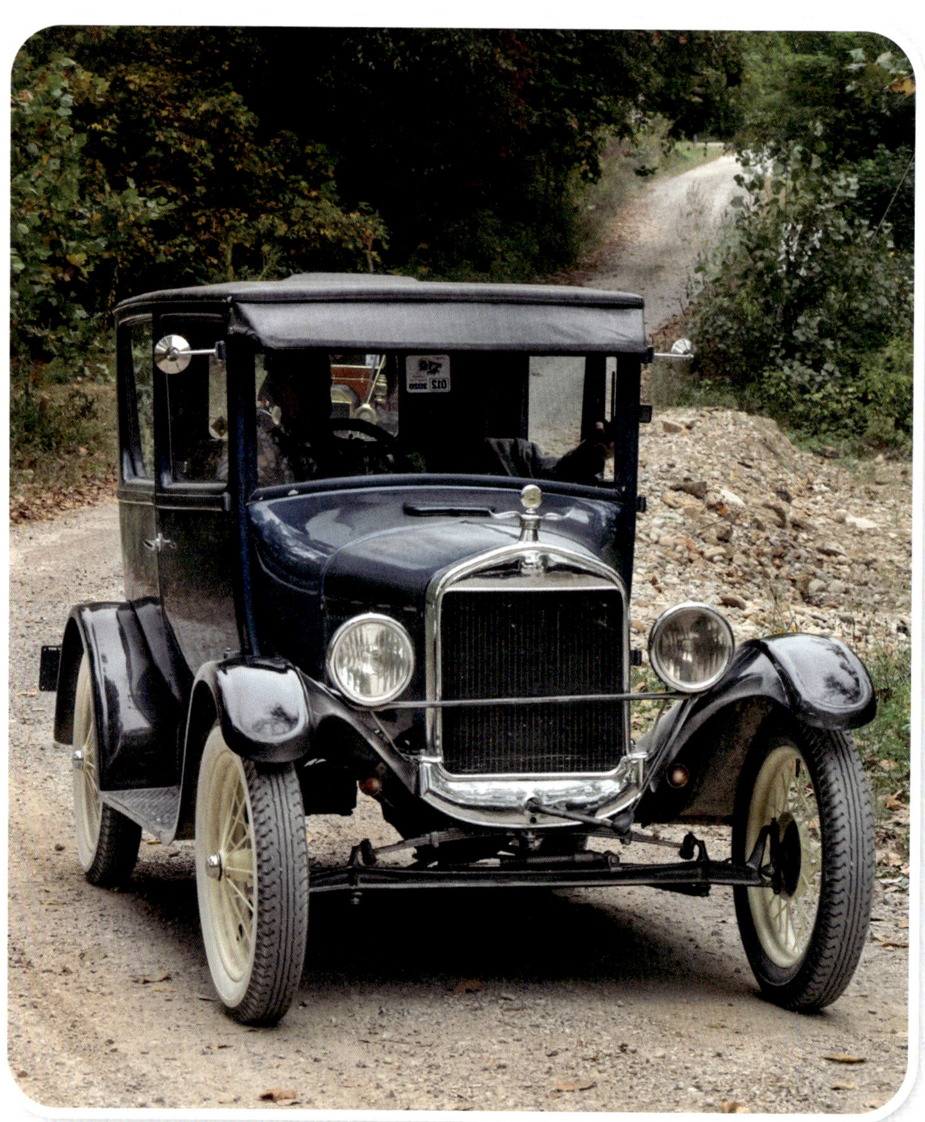

This was a method of making cars where, instead of the engineers moving all their tools from one car to another, the cars carefully moved along a belt to the engineer.

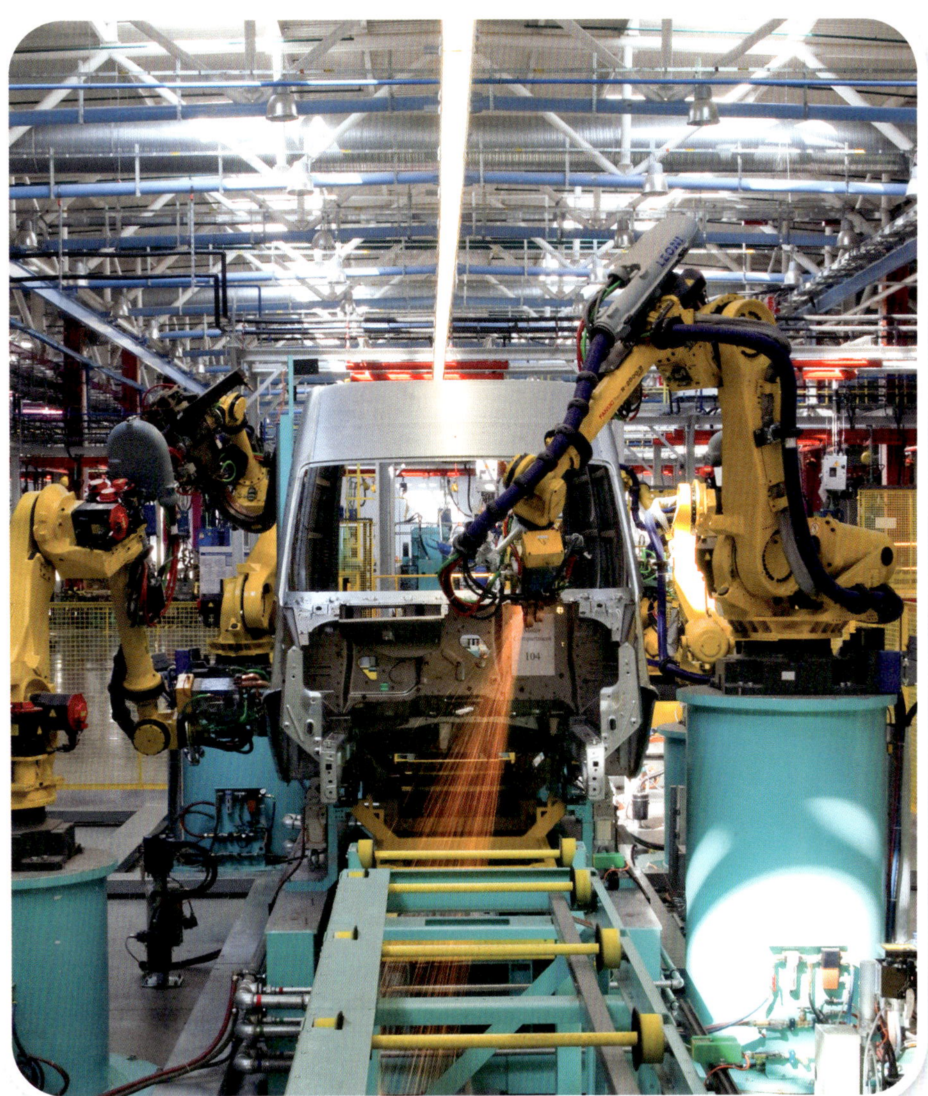

Cars changed a lot about how we do things.
People could travel farther and faster than
they did in the past. People could have
homes farther from where they worked
and travel by car.

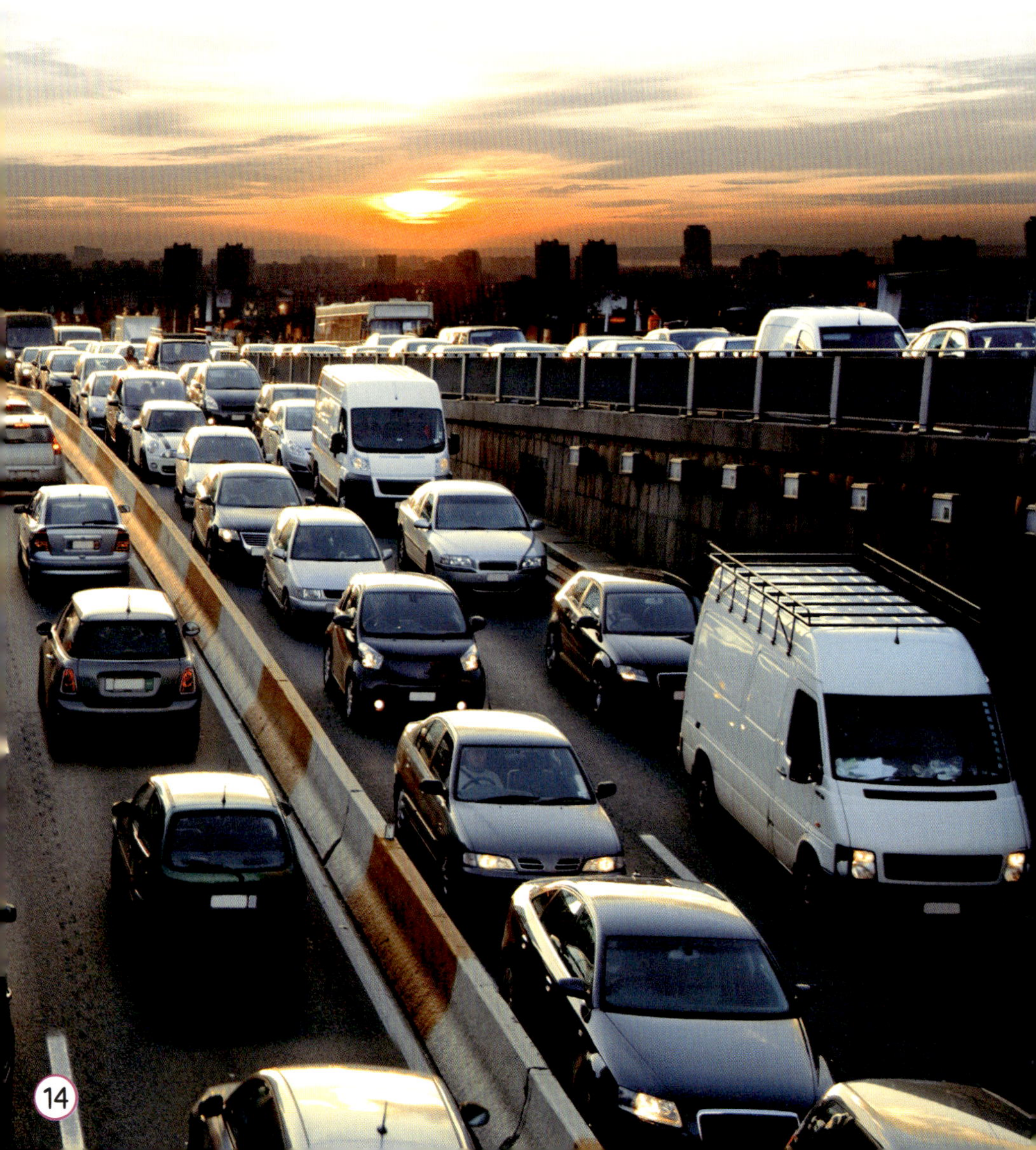

Every city and town has been made and remade with the car in mind. Roads have been cut into landscapes that stood unchanged for thousands of years.

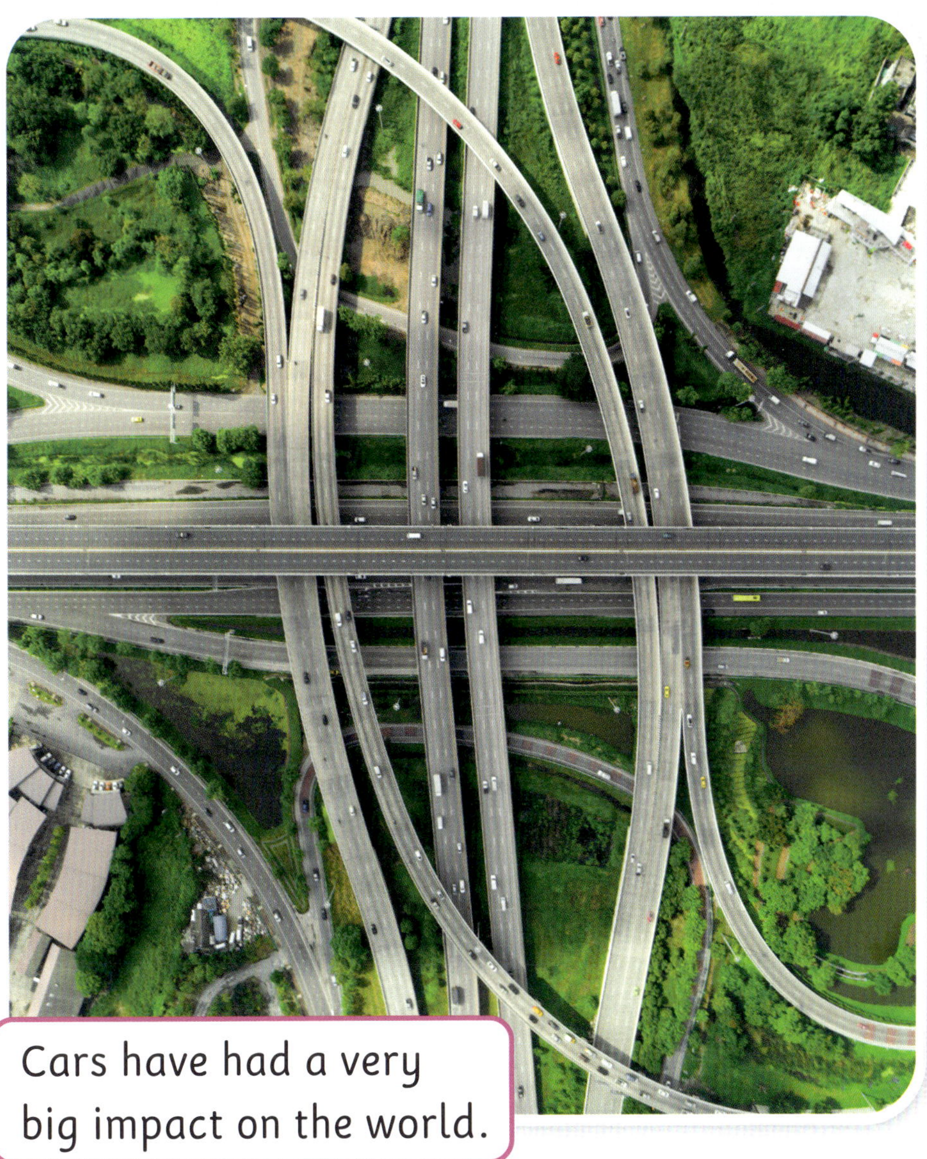

Cars have had a very big impact on the world.

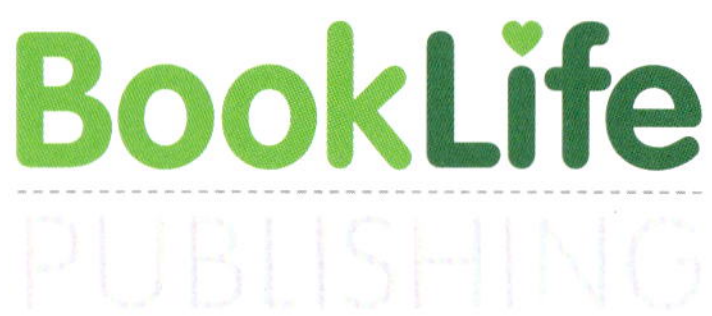

©2022 **BookLife Publishing Ltd.**
King's Lynn, Norfolk, PE30 4LS, UK

ISBN 978-1-80155-813-6

All rights reserved. Printed in Poland.
A catalogue record for this book is available
from the British Library.

How Cars Changed the World
Written by Robin Twiddy
Designed by Drue Rintoul

An Introduction to BookLife Readers...

Our Readers have been specifically created in line with the London Institute of Education's approach to book banding and are phonetically decodable and ordered to support each phase of the Letters and Sounds document.

Each book has been created to provide the best possible reading and learning experience. Our aim is to share our love of books with children, providing both emerging readers and prolific page-turners with beautiful books that are guaranteed to provoke interest and learning, regardless of ability.

BOOK BAND GRADED using the Institute of Education's approach to levelling.

PHONETICALLY DECODABLE supporting each phase of Letters and Sounds.

EXERCISES AND QUESTIONS to offer reinforcement and to ascertain comprehension.

CLEAR DESIGN to inspire and provoke engagement, providing the reader with clear visual representations of each non-fiction topic.

AUTHOR INSIGHT:
ROBIN TWIDDY

Robin Twiddy is one of BookLife Publishing's most creative and prolific editorial talents, who imbues all his copy with a sense of adventure and energy. Robin's Cambridge-based first class honours degree in psychosocial studies offers a unique viewpoint on factual information and allows him to relay information in a manner that readers of any age are guaranteed to retain. He also holds a certificate in Teaching in the Lifelong Sector, and a post graduate certificate in Consumer Psychology.

A father of two, Robin has written many titles for BookLife and specialises in conceptual, role-playing narratives which promote interaction with the reader and inspire even the most reluctant of readers to fully engage with his books.

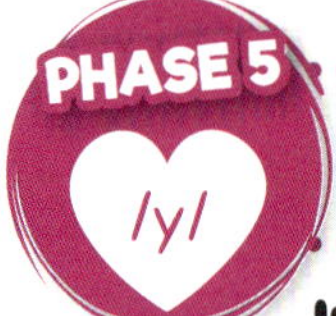

This book focuses on the alternative pronunciations of the grapheme /y/ and is a Purple level 8 book band.